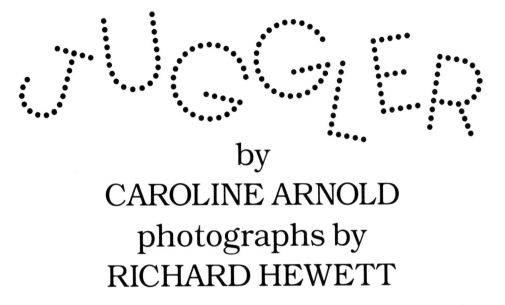

JUGGLER

by
CAROLINE ARNOLD
photographs by
RICHARD HEWETT

Clarion Books

TICKNOR & FIELDS: A HOUGHTON MIFFLIN COMPANY
New York

Acknowledgments

For his invaluable assistance and cheerful coop-
eration we are grateful to Jahnathon Whitfield
of the California Juggling Institute, Santa Ana,
California. We also thank Eddy Rose, Mike Hatal-
ski, Jay Watson, Jennifer Ames, the Pasadena
Public Library and the participants in the 39th
Annual International Jugglers Association
Convention for all their help in this project.

Clarion Books
Ticknor & Fields, a Houghton Mifflin Company
Text copyright © 1988 by Caroline Arnold
Photographs copyright © 1988 by Richard Hewett
All rights reserved.
For information about permission to reproduce
selections from this book, write to Permissions,
Houghton Mifflin Company, 2 Park Street, Boston, MA 02108
Printed in the U.S.A.

Library of Congress Cataloging-in-Publication Data
Arnold, Caroline.
    Juggler.

    Includes index.
    Summary: Text and photographs follow Jahnathon
Whitfield, a professional juggler, as he entertains
audiences, teaches juggling skills, and attends a
jugglers' convention.
    1. Whitfield, Jahnathon—Juvenile literature.
2. Jugglers—Biography—Juvenile literature.
[1. Whitfield, Jahnathon.   2. Jugglers]   I. Hewett,
Richard, ill.   II. Title.
GV1545.W48A76   1988   793.8′092′4 [B] [92]   87-24908
ISBN 0-89919-496-6

H 10 9 8 7 6 5 4 3 2 1

ne, two, three. One, two, three. The spinning clubs twirled high into the air. Over and over they turned, each one tracing a rhythmic pattern in space. Then, as each club fell, the juggler quickly caught it and tossed it up again. It almost seemed like magic the way he was able to keep the clubs moving without ever dropping one.

Jahnathon Whitfield is a professional juggler who performs at schools, libraries, shopping centers, and for parties and groups in his community. His act includes a combination of juggling and balancing tricks as well as games and information about juggling.

During a recent performance at a library, Jahnathon talked to the audience as he did tricks. "Did you know that juggling is a sport that people have been doing since ancient times?" he asked. "On the walls of some tombs in Egypt are pictures of people juggling that are nearly four thousand years old. Nobody knows why the Egyptians juggled. Perhaps they did it for fun or as part of a religious ritual. In any case they are making some of the same juggling moves in the pictures that people use today. The word *juggle* comes from a Latin word meaning "to joke" or "to jest." A juggler is an entertainer who does tricks that fool the eye."

"To become a juggler you need to develop a good sense of balance," said Jahnathon as he picked up his unicycle. "Jugglers in circuses often combine balancing with other juggling tricks. One famous juggler liked to balance a floor lamp on his chin as he held another juggler on his left hand and juggled plates with his right hand."

The students watched in amazement as Jahnathon placed his unicycle on his chin and balanced it. "I practiced a long time before I could do that," he said.

When Jahnathon finished his act, everyone in the audience clapped enthusiastically.

"That looks like fun," the children said. "Can we try it too?"

"It's not as easy as it looks," said Jahnathon. "But I can show you some simple skills that will help you to get started."

He opened his bag of equipment and took out a cluster of peacock feathers. As the children stood up, Jahnathon gave each one a feather.

"This is a simple exercise that will improve both your balance and coordination," said Jahnathon. "First place the bottom of the upright feather in the palm of one hand. Now, try to balance the feather so it doesn't fall."

The children found that they had to move their hands from side to side in order to keep their feather steady.

"The secret," said Jahnathon, "is to keep your eye on the *top* of the feather. Your hand below will move automatically."

Soon most of the children were able to balance the feather, at least for a while.

"After you learn how to balance the feather on your hand, you can try putting it on your chin or nose," suggested Jahnathon.

As Jahnathon put away his equipment, he said, "You can practice balancing at home. If you don't have a feather, you can try a yardstick or a thin dowel. But be sure to practice where you have plenty of room so you won't knock over anything."

He also told them about the class he taught at the community center. "Some people learn to juggle on their own," he said, "but it's more fun to take a class."

The students in Jahn-athon's juggling class at the community center were at several levels. Some already knew the basic juggling moves, and others were be-ginners.

At the start of each class Jahnathon usually demonstrated a new skill or a different kind of juggling equipment. This time he was showing the students how to juggle clubs. Clubs are popular with jugglers because they are easy to catch and throw, and because of their size they are easy for an audience to see. Each time Jahnathon tossed a club he flicked his wrist so that the club turned once before he caught it again.

After the demonstration Jahnathon worked with each class member individually. This time Jahnathon was going to teach Eddy how to juggle scarves.

"The real secret of juggling is timing and coordination," said Jahnathon. "If you learn the correct juggling moves slowly with scarves, it makes it much easier to juggle balls or beanbags later on."

Eddy started with one scarf. "Hold the scarf in the center," said Jahnathon. "Then throw it gently into the air by lifting your wrist upward and across your body. As the scarf falls, catch it with your other hand in a downward motion."

Eddy tried it. Because the scarf was so light, it floated slowly toward the ground, making it easy to catch.

"Good," said Jahnathon. "Now we'll try it with two scarves."

Eddy watched as Jahnathon tossed up the scarf in his right hand. As the scarf reached its peak he tossed the scarf in his left hand into the air. Then he caught the first scarf with his right hand and the second scarf with his left hand. Eddy did the same.

"That's not so hard," he said.

"No," said Jahnathon as he handed him a third scarf. "But now we will add one more step. Hold two scarves in one hand and one in the other," he directed. "Starting with the hand that has two scarves, throw one scarf at a time alternating your tosses and catches like this." Eddy watched while Jahnathon demonstrated. "Try to throw the scarves in the same place each time and develop a steady rhythm," added Jahnathon.

Then Eddy tried it. Toss right. Toss left. Catch left. Toss right. Catch right. Catch left. Then he did it again and again.

"Hey, look at me!" he shouted. "I can do it!"

Jahnathon smiled. "Yes," he said. "Practice at home this week. Next time we'll start with beanbags."

At the beginning of the next class Jahnathon gave Eddy three beanbags.

"The nice thing about beanbags," he said, "is that they are easy to catch, and when you drop them they don't bounce or roll."

They started with just one beanbag. Eddy put it in his right hand.

"Now," said Jahnathon, "hold out your left hand and imagine a point straight above it in front of your shoulder. Try to throw the beanbag so that it stops at that point and then drops into your left hand."

Eddy tossed his beanbag, but he threw too hard and it missed his left hand. He tried again. This time it was not quite far enough.

"I'll help you," said Jahnathon, "by marking your imaginary point. Keep your eye on that point and it will help you to concentrate."

Eddy kept trying and he improved.

"Now do the same thing, throwing with your left hand," said Jahnathon.

Because Eddy was right-handed, he was not used to throwing with his left hand. This action was much harder. He kept trying, but soon the class was over. He would have to practice all week to throw with his left hand as easily as he did with his right.

At the next class Jahnathon showed him how to combine the two skills of throwing with each hand.

"When the beanbag tossed from the right hand reaches the imaginary point over your left shoulder, it is time to toss the left beanbag."

Eddy watched as Jahnathon demonstrated.

"Now you try it," he said.

Eddy soon realized why it was so important to throw evenly with each hand. If he threw one beanbag too high or too low, it was harder to catch and it threw off his rhythm for the next toss.

With a lot of concentration, Eddy was finally able to master throwing two beanbags.

"Now," said Jahnathon, "we'll add a third beanbag and you will learn one of the first real juggling tricks. This is called the three-ball cascade."

Jahnathon placed two beanbags in his right hand and one in the left. Then, starting with his right he tossed each beanbag to the other hand. He waited for each beanbag to reach the imaginary point before tossing the next.

It looked easy, but when Eddy tried it, all his beanbags ended up on the floor. He tried again and again, but with no success.

"This is a lot harder than juggling scarves," moaned Eddy.

"Keep trying," Jahnathon encouraged him, "and you'll be surprised at how fast you will learn."

When the class was over Eddy went home to practice. Jahnathon went home to prepare for the Renaissance Fair the next weekend.

23

The Renaissance Fair was an annual outdoor festival held on a ranch outside the city. For the fair, tents were put up, and booths and stages were constructed along a winding pathway. The buildings were decorated to look as if they were in sixteenth-century England, the time of Queen Elizabeth I. All the food, games, crafts, and entertainment also had a Renaissance theme.

Like many of the fairgoers, Jahnathon wore a costume that looked like what someone might have worn in Elizabethan times. For many people, the fair was an opportunity to spend the day pretending to live in another time and place.

Because juggling was a popular form of entertainment in the Renaissance, many jugglers came to the fair. There was even a booth where jugglers could practice or where people could take lessons.

Jahnathon always enjoyed going to the fair because it was a good chance to observe how other jugglers worked. Some of the jugglers at the fair performed in the middle of the crowds and others worked on small stages. Each juggler had his or her own special tricks, and many jugglers told jokes or funny stories while they performed. Jahnathon found his friend Michael working in front of one of the game booths.

He invited Michael to visit his class at the community center the following week.

28

When Michael came to the class, he brought his juggling equipment with him. He showed the students some variations on three-ball juggling that he had just learned. Michael was using lacrosse balls, and in one pattern, or routine, he bounced one ball rather than tossing it. Then he and Jahnathon demonstrated two person juggling, or passing, with six clubs. Jahnathon explained to the class that although it looked complicated, the moves for two person juggling are very much like those of the three-ball cascade. The only difference is that you throw to your partner rather than to yourself. Again, the key to success is developing good timing and coordination.

Eddy could hardly wait until the demonstration was over so he could tell Jahnathon what he had learned.

"Guess what!" he said. "I can juggle!"

"Let's see," said Jahnathon.

Eddy carefully planted his feet on the ground, making sure he was steady. Then he tossed each of the three beanbags into the air, keeping an even rhythm of toss and catch.

"Wonderful!" said Jahnathon. "You're on your way to becoming a real juggler."

Over the next few weeks Eddy worked on his three-ball cascade. The more he practiced the more confident he became. He also started to juggle other objects. Because clubs are difficult to use at first, Jahnathon suggested that he start by substituting one club for one of his bean-bags. Later on he could add the second and third club.

Jahnathon's classes at the community center would end soon for summer vacation. Over the summer Eddy planned to practice. Perhaps he would put on a small show for the kids in his neighborhood. Then, in the fall, he would come back to learn more.

As with any skill, juggling improves with practice. Even people who have juggled for many years can always learn new tricks or more complicated moves. When Jahnathon is not teaching or performing, he works at expanding the number of tricks he can do and perfecting the difficult ones.

Each year, usually in July, Jahnathon attends the annual week-long jugglers' convention sponsored by the International Jugglers Association. At this yearly meeting hundreds of jugglers from all over the world get together to have fun, to learn from each other, and to have a chance to perform.

The people who come to the jugglers' convention range from beginners to professionals. They are interested in juggling as well as related skills which are often part of a juggler's act. These may include unicycle riding, plate spinning, or hat exchanging.

During the day the jugglers attend workshops where they can learn about specific skills or the use of special equipment. They also go into a gymnasium to practice. In the gymnasium there is plenty of room and a large mirror which helps the jugglers to see how they appear to an audience.

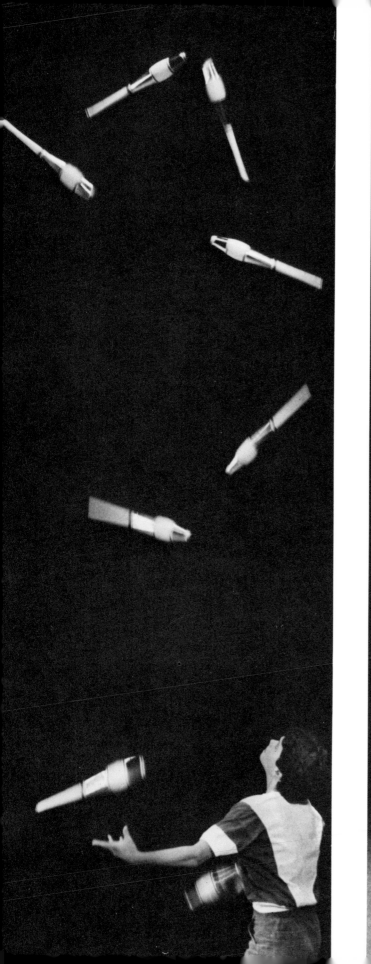

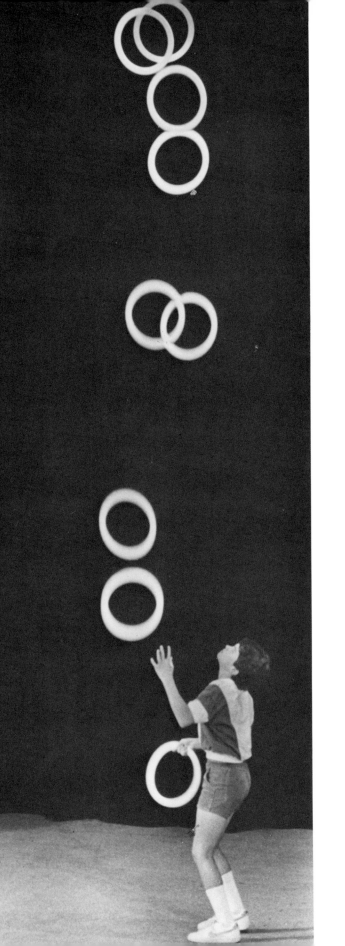

For the very skilled jugglers the convention offers competitions for prizes. In one type of contest, called numbers juggling, the jugglers compete to see who can juggle the most balls, clubs or rings during a given period of time. To juggle many objects, the juggler must toss each one high into the air to allow more time between tossing and catching.

Rings are the easiest to throw in large numbers because they are thin and not as likely to bump into each other as clubs or balls. They are also the easiest to catch.

The convention also sponsors competitions for performers. One afternoon is devoted to street performers, people who specialize in entertaining on street corners, at fairs or in other places where there is no formal stage. Participants put on their acts in a local park. Usually several acts are going on at once. As each performer begins his or her act, a crowd gathers to watch. If the performer is entertaining, the crowd stays; if not, it moves on to the next performer. In these acts the performers often wear colorful costumes, juggle unusual objects, or tell funny stories in order to attract the crowd's attention.

More formal stage performances are held in the evening in a large auditorium. Here the performers also wear costumes and usually coordinate their act with recorded music. There are competitions for people under the age of eighteen, over eighteen, and for juggling teams. To award the prizes, a panel of judges decides who is the best both in juggling skill and presentation.

Jahnathon has mastered many juggling skills, but he does not enter these competitions. Nevertheless, he enjoys watching them and often becomes inspired by them to try new things in his own act.

Although Jahnathon enjoys performing, he prefers to concentrate on teaching and helping other people to learn the joys of juggling. His students include both children and adults.

Today more and more people are learning to juggle. Some enjoy juggling just because it is fun and relaxing. Like any other game or sport, it is a challenge to learn to do it well. Other people juggle for exercise and as a way to develop and improve their coordination. A few people, like Jahnathon, become professional jugglers and earn their living by teaching and performing.

Juggling has always fascinated people. Jugglers can be found in circuses, at fairs, on street corners, at parties, or wherever there is a need for entertainment. The first basic steps of juggling are easy to learn and provide the framework for mastering more complicated tricks. Juggling for either fun or profit is a skill that lasts a lifetime.

46

FOR MORE INFORMATION ABOUT JUGGLING

If you want to learn more about juggling you can write to the International Jugglers Association at Box 29, Kenmore, New York, 14217. They can help you to find out where to get juggling equipment and if there are any juggling associations in your area. Their quarterly magazine includes information about current events in juggling as well as practical advice. You might also ask your local park or recreation center if any juggling classes are being offered in your area.

A catalogue of juggling equipment and information about juggling programs may also be obtained by sending a stamped, self-addressed envelope to the California Juggling Institute, 15651 Eden(J), Westminster, California 92683.

Two helpful books about learning how to juggle are *Juggling Is for Me* by Nancy Marie Temple and Rande Aronson (Lerner, 1986) and *How to Be a Juggler* by Charles R. Meyer (David McKay, 1977).

INDEX